MW00695310

# Land of The Living

Ashlee Haze

To: Ashley Kay
You are a light and
#blackgirlsrock

Ashlee Haze

Ashlee Haze

Copyright © 2016 by Ashlee Haze

All rights reserved. This book or any portion thereof may not be reproduced or used in any manner whatsoever without the express written permission of the publisher except for the use of brief quotations in a book review. For permission requests, write to the publisher, addressed "Attention: Permissions Coordinator," at the email address below:
info@ashleehaze.com

Printed in the United States of America First Printing, 2016


ISBN: 0-9973168-0-2
ISBN-13: 978-0-9973168-0-3

Cover Art By: Daryl Funn
Editor: Anïsa Lewis

I remain confident of this: I will see the goodness of the LORD in the land of the living. Psalm 27:13

# CONTENTS

## i. Grief

## ii. Talitha Koum (Life Goes On)    25

# ACKNOWLEDGMENTS

My grandmother once said, "People don't have to be nice to you. When they are, the least you could do is say 'thank you.' " That old wisdom was my first lesson in gratitude and I am better for it.

My first "Thank You" is always to God and this great universe. To have been granted the gifts of poetry and words is something I don't take lightly. I will use it until I'm empty.

Kim Nelson: You are my first home and my rock in times of need. You rejoice with me through everything. How blessed I am to have a mother who loves me and cultivates me daily. Sometimes words fail me when it comes to thanking you, and it is my hope that the life I live is an honor to you.

Jaylen and Jacari: When I asked God for responsibility he gave me two little brothers. This world doesn't always know how to value men like you. I will guard you two with my life.

Grandma Winnie: Thank you for always reminding me that "time brings about change." Although it has indeed changed us, it has never changed your love for me.

Goddaddy: Thank you for being the true essence of a godparent. Thank you for stepping up to the plate when my father passed. You have made me a better person.

GG and all my other aunts, uncles, and cousins: My family stretches from sea to shining sea. Anywhere I am is home because of you.

Vernon Nelson: You have gone to be with the ancestors but you haven't stopped parenting. I feel your presence in my life every day.

Hunter: Some people spend their whole lives searching for a soul mate. Mine sat next to me in 9th grade German class and has been by my side ever since. Thank you for teaching me so much about love and all that it requires. Thank you for being my #1 fan. You make the scariest moments seem small.

Shanel: You are more than my friend. You are my sister. You taught me how to use eyeliner and you are literally always one call away. I have more memories with you than I can count. We have many more to make.

Contessa: In the span of my life, you and I have been friends longer than we haven't. 15 years and you are still as true as day one. Thank you for always having my back.

Kelundra & Morgan: Our trio has been my saving grace. If I had a dollar for every happy hour, brunch, lunch, dinner, show, or just plain foolish idea we've had, we'd all be rich. It is at those restaurant tables and in those seats that we became women.

My Love: Thank you for putting up with me and my shenanigans. Thank you for not letting me sleep an extra 5 minutes. Thank you for telling me when I'm not working hard enough. Thank you for your patience. I can be hard to love at times, but you do it anyway.

The Atlanta Poetry Scene: Thank you for molding me into the poet I am. Thank you Java Monkey Slam for being my poetry home. Thank you to the vets who helped me along the way- Georgia Me, Abyss, Jon Goode, Cola, Cocktails. You wrote the blueprint. I'm just building.

Poetry Slam, Inc.: Thank you for outlets such as the National Poetry Slam, Women of the World Poetry Slam, and the Individual Poetry Slam. The slam community has always welcomed me with open arms and for that, I am grateful. Thank you Southern Fried family for always providing a safe space.

Thank you to everyone who bought a chapbook or CD. Thank you to everyone who watched my videos, re-tweeted my work, and liked my statuses. It is the highest honor to know that you heard me.

Thank you (yes, you) for reading this work which is so near and dear to me. I hope this work inspired by grief and what it is to still live on inspires you and speaks to you in some way. This is the most cathartic thing I have to offer.

# Grief

"So it's true, when all is said and done, grief is the price we pay for love."
— E.A. Bucchianeri, Brushstrokes of a Gadfly

## this spot just won't come out

my father died
and every morning I wake up with grief outstretched
covering me like an extra blanket
grief dripping down the walls
grief rising from my clothes like cheap perfume
grief stuck under my shoes like stepped-in gum
grief in the crevices of my teeth
grief spilled on the rug i just bought
this grief--
this rugged thing--
it is ugly all over
and I got it all over everything

## lazarus

when Lazarus fell sick Mary and Martha ran to Jesus to tell him the news.
they were expecting a miracle.
Jesus, in his infinite wisdom, sent them back to Bethany.
when the news came that Lazarus had passed, Mary and Martha ran to
Jesus and lamented
"had you been here then he would not have died!"
Jesus replied, "don't you know he had to die in order for me to perform a
miracle? after all, where's the magic in giving life to the living?"
so Jesus went to the tomb where Lazarus lay
and commanded him, "rise up and walk!" and he did.
that day, Lazarus became a living testimony that even death can't stop a
miracle.

when my father fell sick, I ran to Jesus to tell him the news.
*I was expecting a miracle.*
Jesus, in his infinite wisdom, sent me back to where I'd come from.
when news came that my father had passed, I ran to Jesus and lamented
"had you been here then he would not have died!"
Jesus replied, "Don't you know he had to die in order for me to perform a
miracle?"
but to my dismay, when he came it was not my father he rose from the
dead, but the parts of myself I had buried with him.
I had amputated the parts of myself I thought I could live without
reasoning that I could not be whole
and I heard a voice say to me
"did you not think that I could still raise you from the dead?
did you, in your finite wisdom, think that just because I waited two years to
come that I would not make a miracle out of you?
yes, your Daddy is dead, but your Father yet lives.
RISE UP AND WALK!
open up your lockjaw mouth and release the winged creatures you have
trapped in your chest!
you can still be a poem though he is not here!"
I did not know I could still be a poem when he is not here
I did not know what to be now that he is not here
the Mary and Martha in me did not think I could still be a miracle
but here I stand, 4 years later.
the stone rolled away from the tomb.
if you look closely you can still see remnants of bandages on my hands and
feet, you can still smell the scent of the grave in my clothes

but know that I am living now.
not even death can stop this miracle.

## haiku #1

black girl magic: see
how she disappears after
routine traffic stop

**when a pen becomes a weapon against yourself and** ~~Freddie Gray~~
**Sandra Bland is still dead**

black poet tip #1
if you wait until the last day of submissions
you can always add another name to your list poem about dead black bodies

**the casket contrapuntal *or* the wife my mother never stopped being**

my mother has always been a certain woman
  *what do you think about the blue with the silver trim?*
always had a knack for the details
  *make sure that button is straight, okay?*
she signs on all the dotted lines, her signature a hymn I know by heart
  *yes, I'll take responsibility for the charges*
but something in this song is a first Sunday communion
  *do you think he would like that?*
it is a taking of blood wine and bread bodies
  *the font is wrong in all the worst ways*
it is the burden of being chosen while wishing not to be
  *there is no one else who can do this*
but look how she dances when she thinks no one is watching
  *there is no one else I will let do this*
look at the balm oozing from her bones
  *there is therapy in this aching chaos*
she is my pomegranate promise in this land of the living
  *there is healing in this rugged moment*
my mother is the tea Ruth drank in the morning
  *there is something necessary in the choosing*
nothing unfaithful lives here
  *know that this will not make a martyr out of me*

## what looks like church on a saturday night

I know what it is to be an unheard prayer
to be the whisper under the orange glow of the streetlights
to be a black body when the gunshots ring
and the sirens blast
to see the black body before it turns blue
before the boys in blue come
before his mother sees the shell of a boy she once carried
we are always there, aren't we?
we lovers of boys who are magic
and disappear just like our fathers taught them
we women, who bring the bandages and the salt
and the tears and the flowers
when there are no flowers, we bring ourselves
and we unlearn love every time they are taken away
the chariots made of blue lights or black bodies always take them
away, don't they?
but they don't see the wound it leaves in us, do they?
they don't hear the earthquake it makes of our wombs, do they?
they do not see us drinking the blood and breaking the body, do
they?
to the women, I need you to know this:
you are the hallelujah that lives off 93rd street
you are a third day rising in the morning
you are what home has always been
*I SEE YOU*
when you feel invisible
*I SEE YOU*
when the city is dark
*I SEE YOU*
and I have never beheld anything more beautiful

## haiku #2

I am not bitter
at your love. I am just
mourning the loss of mine

**what to do when she asks you why we broke up**

1. Decide whether or not to lie or tell the truth. If you choose to lie, stop here. Save this for the one who is worth it.
2. Tell her something generic like, "we had our differences." If she believes you, stop here. Save this for the one who is worth it.
3. Call me a bitch at least once during the conversation. It will make you feel better. It will make *her* feel better.
4. Remember every argument we had leading up to the break up. This will be easier if I am the villain.
5. Tell her the truth: that I wanted a man to love me the way I wanted to be loved. What I had was a man who loved me the best way he knew how.
6. Tell her I decided that was not enough.
7. Tell her the truth: that I was only your 3rd beer[1].
8. She will then know that she is the 4th. Let her be enough, the one thing you wouldn't let me be.
9. Make love to her. She will assume this means you belong to her. Let your body do the lying for you.
10. When the morning sun kisses your face and you roll over, if she is still there, gather all of the pieces of yourself I didn't return and give them to her. This will have to be enough.

---

[1] After Toni Morrison's *Song of Solomon*: "She was the third beer. Not the first one, which the throat receives with almost tearful gratitude; nor the second, that confirms and extends the pleasure of the first. But the third, the one you drink because it's there, because it can't hurt, and because what difference does it make?"

## haiku #3

love life résumé :
good job, no kids, but too fat
for an interview

## questions asked over dinner

what is said:
when are you going to ~~straighten~~ fix your hair?
does your boyfriend still do ~~field~~ construction work?
don't you think you can do ~~richer~~ better?
~~aren't you tired of being fat?~~ want to go on this diet with me?
but you're such a smart girl.

what I ~~think~~ hope they are trying to say:
this is the world we live in
I want you to be happy, and what I think to be happy is everything you are
not
I thought the only things a fat, black, dark-skinned girl could be
are sad
and sorry
and compromise
and you, honey, are anything but

*they do not know that these questions are an act of violence*
*I do not know how to tell them of the war they have made out of me*

## dreams of ice water while living in hell

and then the god of straight parts and laid edges came to me and said
"do not be afraid
for it is I that carries the soul from the black body right before it hits
the ground
and it is I that gives sleep to the mother
there is always red kool-aid in heaven
and black bodies can be black bodies here
there is always a bone thugz song playing at the pearly gates
and everybody takes off their chalk outline before entering
big mamma always has a pot of greens on
and your spades partner never, I mean never, reneges.
don't you believe in a paradise like this?
don't you believe that there is more to the afterlife
than pain and grief and a white man telling your mother what you could
have done not to die?"

# Talitha Koum (Life Goes On)

He went in and said to them, "Why all this commotion and wailing? The child is not dead, but asleep." He took her by the hand and said to her, "Talitha koum!" (which means "Little girl, I say to you, get up!"). Immediately the girl stood up and began to walk around. At this they were completely astonished. Mark 5:41 & 43

**because there must be some reason other than yourself**

you not like the rest of them
you well spoken, you great test scores
you house among fields
I mean...you should be grateful
all that dark
all that sheep wool hair
and they still want you in the club
you ought to get a haircut
ought to buy a new suit
ought to tuck all that motherland away in public
ought to be only behind the hyphen
better leave your Africa at home
it will be here when you get back
better show them white boys
better show them black boys
that you ain't like them
that you different
because you must be different
must be some kind of commodity
must be novel
must be taxidermy over the dean's office door
must be trophy
I mean, why else would they let you in?

## haiku #4

tell the stories of
girls who have chocolate for skin
and cotton for hair

## shake what the motherland gave you

he said "real women don't twerk."
oh really? the last time I checked, what I do with my backside
don't make me hold my head any less high
I remember before you called it twerkin'
me and my cousins would "pop" in the backyard at family reunions
and it didn't make us any less women
I remember watching my mother and her sisters move their hips
like there was freedom in their bones and it didn't make them any less
goddess
we have been shaking our backsides since before we knew what foreign soil
tasted like
back home, called it mapouka, called it kukere
called it sacrifice for the gods
and I will present my offering every time I hear
"cash money records taking over for the 99 and the two thousand"
I will not let you tell me that the Africa in my back is something that I
should be ashamed of
I will not let you tell me it is something I should hide
I will shake it for all the world to see
it is mine
it is mine
it is mine.

## the etymology of negus

you will demand we learn how to say
gorbechev
da vinci
saint laurent
dostoevsky
dicaprio
you will demand we say them right
but will insist that Quvenzhané
demands too much of the tongue and lips
you will say our cousins' names
and spit them out like it leaves a bad taste in the back of the throat
you will ask my brother can you call him ~~Toby~~ Jay for short
beg our mothers to take back the first gift they ever gave us
and I will say every time
say our names correctly with every part of your mouth
say our names the way our mothers intended you to say them
I do not give you permission to chop off the parts that make you
uncomfortable
there are parts of you that make me uncomfortable
and yet you are still here

### haiku #5

how privileged you
are that you can say "home" and
know where that place is

## haiku #6

forgive yourself for
not being who or what you
thought you'd be by now

## NEA ONNIM NO SUA A, OHU

today I am burning sage and drinking hibiscus tea
I have youtubed 10 ways to wrap a head wrap
and still managed to wrap an 11th on my own head
it has been 5 years since I returned to natural
and my mom is still asking me what I plan to do with my hair
    *I am still getting used to telling her "it IS done!"*
today I am slathering this melanin in mango scented Shea butter
and daring you to call it anything but the sun
I have started summoning my ancestors
after years of thinking this practice witchcraft
    *who named it that anyway?*
I am naming myself again in Adinkra symbols
picking fresh flowers to make a crown of
today I am reclaiming all of the things I thought I didn't have a right
to
    *can you believe that?*
    *an African who didn't think she had a right to Africanness?*
I am still learning that even though I was stolen from my mother
I am STILL heir to her fortune
    *this is me reminding myself of this*
the ackee tree bears fruit for me in a language I have to re-learn
a tongue you thought I would never go back to find
I am going back for EVERYTHING that was stolen from me
    *some things you think are yours are still mine*
remember that if nothing else
some things you think are yours have always been mine

Ashlee Haze

**haiku #7**

I am only a
budding fruit, but the roots are
firmly planted here

**The Help**

"you is smart, you is kind, you is important."
Nicole Parker, a New York blogger, has reasoned that
"Black women across America should be outraged at the depiction of maids
in the new film, *The Help*."
I stare at my computer screen and think, "outraged about what?"
the only people ever offended by the truth are those, when given the
choice, prefer the lie.
I find this movie to be extremely nostalgic.
It reminds me of my grandmother, who cleaned houses by day and was a
hotel maid by night.
reminds me of picture my mother showed me of her grandmother's house
in Mississippi.
the floors shined in the photographs.
She reminds me
"we didn't have much, but it was always clean."
this film reminds me of Saturday mornings spent earning my right to go
outside
back when children had to earn their right to go outside.
"are the baseboards clean?!" my mother would ask
as if anyone but her ever noticed a dirty baseboard anyway.
this film reminds me that cleanliness is next to godliness
and I come from a line of broom toting angels.
Ms. Parker...
WHAT WERE YOU EXPECTING?
this ain't no ancestry.com commercial.
this is the story of history at it's finest.
the story of women who kept their prayers in their apron pockets
and sprinkled them in dinner so the children they raised would know love
even after they were gone.
women who know 101 ways to use crisco.
women who knew school as somewhere they'd been once upon a time but
could never go back
because 90 cents an hour keeps bellies full and clothes on backs.
what upsets me is that you, like too many people I know,
think that this history is something to be ashamed of.
it's okay to be a daughter of the holocaust, okay to have walked the trail of
tears
noble to have the blood of Cesar Chavez in your veins
but you be damned if you be black.
my knowledge of my ancestors may only span 200 years,

but I am proud to be the daughter of martyrs, of Mississippi maids and Birmingham marchers.
you laugh at our grandmothers for getting your language wrong.
they were just trying to make do with the stolen pieces they were given.
on May 6, 2012 I graduated from Georgia State University
and it was a tribute to the women who cleaned houses so that I would have to.
who served coffee quietly so that I could be a poet.
it will be for Geraldine Harris, Ophelia McGinnis, Aunt Essy, Aunt Katie, and Aunt Annie
so they know I don't take it for granted.
what upsets me
is that you make fun of the mantra my grandmother's spirit speaks to me everyday:
"you is smart, you is kind, and you is important."

**for the white man who touched my hair in a backwoods north carolina cracker barrel**

tell the truth
if we were not here in this public place
what else would you have touched without asking?

**heroes**

Africa has always been enough for herself
it was you who needed saving

### the origin of a monster

the little boy who breaks the toy he is told he cannot have
or punches the little girl that beats him in a race
grows up to be the man who stabs a woman who refuses his advances
he is the "nice kid" you laughingly told your friends
*just wouldn't take no for an answer*

## citation

I sit back and watch white queer men
who think they invented our wheel
the black woman was always first
and last,
and in the shadows of a death drop
remember to cite us in your works

**plague**

depression has always been this thing other people "get"
something I couldn't possibly have
then one day I realized there was no lamb's blood on this doorpost
when it invited itself in for coffee
and stuck around for lunch

## re-gifting

"out of all the motherland names you could choose
all the names with vowels that open the throat like a sliding door
the names you knew were abandoned at shore
the names that demand your tongue dance
why would you not change it?"

dear black fist
dear dashiki
dear vegan, gluten free brotha selling incense in the West End
I have kept this name
because it is the name my mother gave me
who am I to give it back?

## for colored girls who don't need Katy Perry when Missy Elliott is enough

3rd grade. I'm in the hallway, when I'm sure I shouldn't have been, and
Cory White comes up to me and asks, "yo! have you heard that new Missy
Elliot track?"
I reply, "who is Missy Elliot!?!"
at the time, my parents only let me listen to the gospel and the smooth jazz
station
but that day...I went home, ran upstairs to my room
and closed the door (a cardinal sin in a black mother's house)
and waited on TRL to come on.
then it happened. metallics and a black trash bag fill my TV screen
and I hear the coolest thing I'd ever heard in 8 years of living
*beep beep, who got the keys to my jeep... Vrooooommm!*
at that moment, I had my entire life figured out:
I was going to grow up to be Missy Elliott.
I spent the next decade of my life recording and rewinding videos to learn
dance moves
passing that dutch
getting my freak on
and trying to figure out what the hell she was saying in "Work It."
there were so many artists I could have idolized at the time
*but Missy was the only one who looked like me*
it is because of Melissa Elliott
that I believed that a fat black girl from Chicago
could dance until she felt pretty
could be sexy and cool
could be a woman playing a man's game
and be unapologetically fly.
If you ask me why representation in the media is important
I will show you the tweet of a black teenager
asking who this "new" artist is that Katy Perry brought out on stage at the
Super Bowl
I will show you my velour Adidas sweat suit and white fur Kangol I begged
my parents for
I will show you a 26 year old woman who learned to dance until she felt
pretty.
feminism wears a throwback jersey, bamboo earrings, and a face beat for
the gods.
feminism is Missy, Da Brat, Lil Kim, Angie Martinez, and Left Eye on the
"Not Tonight" track.
feminism says as a woman in my arena, you are not my competition.

as a woman in my arena, your light doesn't make mine any dimmer.

Dear Missy,
I did not grow up to be you
but I did grow up to be me
and to be in love with who this woman is.
to be a woman playing a man's game
and not be apologetic about any of it.
if you ask me why representation is important
I will tell you that on the days I don't feel pretty
I hear the sweet voice of Missy singing to me:
*pop that pop that, jiggle that fat*
*don't stop, get it til your clothes get wet*
I will tell you that right now there are a million
black girls just waiting to see someone who looks like them.